Sincerely

Kaylie Do

BookLeaf Publishing

Presentation by *BookLeaf Publishing*

Web: www.bookleafpub.com

E-mail: info@bookleafpub.com

ISBN: 9789357745215

First edition 2023

*To my family, friends, and everyone who
has shaped me into who I am today.*

Home

A place of laughter
With smiles galore
Full of warmth and comfort
Couldn't ask for more

A place of tears
Frustration abundant
Where parents lecture
Children seethe and vent

A place of despair
People change and leave
Friends grow apart
The old bliss seems naive

A place of light
friends gather to meet
Pressure is gone
It's fun and upbeat

A place of belonging
Where you learn and grow
With people who care
So just relax, take it slow

Father

To what shall I compare
My father who loves and cares
With eyes full of light
Smiles, warm and bright
I simply hope this simple poem
Can make my gratitude known
Or at least be enough to say
To my father,
Your love I could never repay

You think of family, even when you tire
To have that thoughtfulness, I always aspire
You buy mother strawberry and tea
And knick knacks to fill us with glee
You have the energy of a child
But are still a parent, tender and mild
And I hope, together we may stay
So for years, I can still say
To my father
Your love, I hope to repay

Thinking now of my future far ahead
I often imagine the kind of man I'll wed
And i hope he'll be just like you

Strong, clever, and true
A righteous man through and through
A playful father for children too
So in the future, little ones will say
To our grandfather
How could we ever repay

So with that I'll close
Before you begin to doze
Thank you for all the years past
And the future years approaching fast
For teaching me everything you know
And being the best example you can show
I loved you every moment then and still today
So one more time I'll say
Your love to me, I could never repay

Mother

Eyes full of light
 And constantly discerning
 Heart flowing with love
 But for love, always yearning

Lips always ready
To soothe with a kiss
Always ready to advise
Mistakes can't be missed

Mind and faith strong
A perfect role model
My support every time
Your lead, I'll try to follow

First you were perfection
You could do no wrong
But then I saw your flaws
You were human all along

My inspiration, my joy
My caretaker since birth
My mother, I thank you
For showing me what I'm worth

A Little Companion

"You're gonna have a brother"
I stared blankly at my mother
I was barely turning three
What fun could a sibling be?

"You're gonna have a brother"
My heart was a-flutter
A new friend seemed exciting
Little did I know there'd be constant fighting

I met my new brother
Three things I've discovered
Babies are loud, kids are a mess
As for kindness, he is the best

My first little companion
With whom I shared everything
Our own exclusive memories
Nostalgia, they'd always bring

It was an interesting time growing up
But our time was filled with love
Our memories filled with laughter
It was a good time thereafter

Having a younger brother
Has definitely made me tougher
But you've shown me to be selfless
a better sister for the next

A Little More Company

"You're gonna have a sister"
This time, I was prepared
But i was still a little scared
Of the responsibilities to come

She was a baby
I got to hold and feed her
She let me dote on and treat her
I thought it'd be fun

The responsibility came
Role model, babysitter, friend
Someone on whom she could depend
I tried my best for her

Sometimes it'd be hard
We clashed as she grew
So I wonder if she knew
I loved her as much as could be

But another girl was exciting
Talk of makeup, books, and boys
Together, we'd make lots of noise
As we argued, laughed, and bonded

My partner in crime
My favorite little buddy
I think we can agree
As much as I've shown you,
You've also taught me

Perfect Pressure

When you have everything
To be grateful for
Is it selfish
To ask for, to want for more

Having much
Means giving much more
The position of role model
Turned into a chore

Perfection at home
For the siblings to see
Perfection at school
For friends relying on me

People push you down
When you build yourself up
But will judge and judge
If you don't do enough

I needed a break
Guilt got in the way
I was burning out
couldn't push duties away

Was it wrong to ask for more
Selfish to want relief
When I was given everything
Except someone to tell me

I never needed to be perfect

Leaving

Is there a pain greater
 Than a friend turned hater
When the one you held dear
Is no longer near
And when feelings turn cold
As a friend disappears

The past "I love you"s
How could they have been true
And our hugs and our smiles
Were you faking it all the while
Because our warmth turned cold
And you disappeared

I gave you all I had
And for a while I was glad
That someone understood
And supported as best they could
Until it simply stopped
And the peace disappeared

But what hurts the most
Is that I'd still hold you close
The second you came back
I'd hide all the cracks

That our relationship held
And pretend you were always here

Even though I felt wronged
Your impact stays strong
Our memories, I'll hold dear
Even if you're not near
And I hope we'll meet again
If you need me, I'll be here

Smile

When "acting" as defense
In a world devoid of sense
The mask we wear
The lies we share
To make a smile
That's not our own

I'm fine, how are you
Has that "fine" ever been true?
That facade we always wear
Because no one seems to care
That we don't have a smile
Of our own

Need I mention the stress
From nights without rest
And for others, constant worry
Till our self esteem be blurry
And only to disguise, would we smile
On our own

They say to share and vent
When ur energy has been spent
But judging remarks you'll hear
From the friends you thought dear

When you show what's behind the smile
That fake smile you own

At this point you're tired
Once your last bit of hope has expired
You sit completely alone
After to the whole world, you've shown
That one beautiful smile
That beautiful, fake smile of your own

Where Did Everyone Go

I try to smile but I look around
And no one else is there
Is it possible that with so many people
Finding friends is rare

I really don't want to bother you
I know it'd be better if I wasn't here
the constant feeling of being alone
Is one of my greatest fears

My goal in life
Is to make others as happy as can be
Is it so wrong to wish
That there was someone like that for me

Someone I don't have to hide around
Or would let me happy for myself
Someone who would make me laugh
And to me, would always know what to tell

But anyone who came close
Always ends up leaving
So who do I turn to for help
When I need comfort for grieving

I sit many days alone
Thinking about the people I know
Why did everyone leave?
Left me feeling so low

But I put on a smile
So that they would be okay
So that they don't feel guilty
When I'm crying at the end of the day

I try to be fine on my own
But sometimes the pain hurts so
I just want to find support
But where did everyone go?

Going on Alone

Tick

Tick

Tick

The clock continues on and on
Time travels til done
Speeds by until it's gone

Go to school
With your mind as tired as could be
Pressured with people to please
Hardly have time to rest or sleep

Go to practice
Because colleges need to know
That you've outshined your peers
Even if it's for show

Go change the world
But be humble
everyone around
Will want you to crumble

Open your messages, open your apps
Turn on your camera and put on a mask

When will it stop, when will it end
The anxiety suffocates and it spreads
It starts in your stomach, reaches your head
Your mind is running and running till it goes-

BEEP BEEP
click

The alarm turned off
get out of bed

Overworking, Overthinking

How can something so gentle
Be dreadful the next
How can the peace and quiet
Have such sorrowful effects

The mind is a weapon
When thoughts run and run
Dreaming the worst
Overthinking's never done

who can understand
Who is there to tell
When divulging makes them judge
But hiding makes you dwell

everyone hates me
our mind becomes convincing
no one understands
Our self worth starts thinning

From smiling in public
To crying in bed
Healing feels impossible
When your emotions are dead

It's effects are heartbreaking
The deafening silence that is
When one is left alone
Left curled up in tears

Relief

While everyone else was leaving
I was able to meet you
Who gave me a place to confide in
And excitement I never knew

How could I help it
With your sweet words and smiles
You consoled me with care
And I fell in love all the while

After a few months I realized
Just how much trouble I was in
no matter how much I denied it
Love was growing quickly within

We joked around in class
And shared our stories till 3
I was constantly stressed for others
But now I felt so free

You don't know how happy it made me
When you confessed your love that June
I was hoping to grow closer slowly
I didn't know it'd be that soon

How lucky and blessed I am
To have a companion such as you
Who cares for me so genuinely
And respects my wishes too

I hope you never forget
That I love you dearly
And simply making you happy
is my greatest wish, sincerely

I can never repay you
For saving me when I needed help most
And accepting me
When I needed someone close

So to my love I hope you'll never forget
I love you more than I can ever say
My God given gift from the beginning
For you, I'm still grateful today

My Love

Since the day is ending
 To you, i'm sending
 Another poem of words
 With sentiments often heard
 But i hope you remember
 I love you more than you'll ever know

You always love to tease
 Will always do as you please
 But somehow, with you i don't mind
 And i constantly seem to find
 That i'm falling in love
 More in love than we'll ever know

With eyes like forests vast
 It's no wonder i fell so fast
 And sweet embraces which stop time
 Between sweet words that claim "mine"
 Again, it's no wonder i love you so
 More than you'd ever know

My darling, my love
 My gift from heavens above
 How happy time would be spent

If every waking moment meant
That i'd be near you forever
No more worries or endeavors
My only work being to love you even if
I love you more than we'll ever know

Friends

To the first one who stayed
Who made me feel important
No matter how we've changed
Time with you is time well spent

You were a ray of light
When I needed it most
Now you're a safe haven
Always meant to be held close

To the one who kept me confident
Who let me be myself
We still have many things to do
So many ideas on our shelf

You're an inspiration
A person I aspire to be
I hope I can one day repay you
For all that you've given me

To the one who changed my life
showed me what peace could be
If only your perception of yourself
Could be the version I see

You made me feel loved
Like I had somewhere to belong
And if I ever fell short
You'd help right my wrongs

What could be more precious
Than people who love and care
For you, they'd do their best
Their compassion, beyond compare

New Relationships

An intended distraction
Became a great relief
Where relationships thrived
Although they were brief

A break from the drama
Of forced friendships outside
A break from the solitude
From having to hide

Labor is easy
With good people around
Moments became memories
The best memories I've found?

The chime of the door
Timers in the kitchen
The sweet smell of syrups
And food cooking on ignition

The rush of the morning
workplace bubbling with excitement
Everyone rushing to assist
All focused on the assignments

The warm peace of the night
Leaving time to chat
Strangers became friends
If only this would last

But alas, all good things end
Of course, lest they be tainted
So must friendships drift
Even with these newly acquainted

Still, good people have a way
Of making their impact remain
This moment can't last forever, but
I hope we'll meet again

Opening Up

How to describe
 That of which cannot be
 That tremendous bliss
 To the soul that is unseen
 when you distance yourself
 From the ones you hold dear
 But they stay to rid burdens
 And dry all your tears

 They'll drag you out
 Help you up
 You're reluctant
 It's so abrupt
 The heart is heavy
 From burying feelings
 "Everyone else is busy
 Everyone else needs healing"

 But people are persuasive
 You start confessing
 All the pain and grief
 That you've been repressing
 Your hands may shake
 But keep going
 Tears may drop

Just keep going

The heart is free
Your mind is light
Going on feels easier
You're finally alright
For what better remedy
Could there be
Than being loved
When you're in need

Lessons Learned

It is inevitable
 That bad events should cascade
 But good ones do as well
 They're simply self-made

There's no point in changing
For those who won't stay
There's no point in rearranging
Oneself without repay

Losing yourself
ends up in pain
all those efforts
Just makes one drained

So it's effective
And much simpler too
To stay oneself
And to oneself, be true

Sincere

My parents' love
 Was selfless and sure
 I was free to be a child
 But learned to be mature

My siblings' love
Was rough but innocent
No matter how we'd clash
Our bond couldn't be bent

My family's love
Was protective but tough
Their affection, boundless
But the judging felt too much

My friends' love
Is of a bittersweet kind
The sweet ones feel short
But they're the best you'll find

My boyfriends love
Was accepting and constant
No matter our struggles
Efforts were always well-meant

My own love
Is still struggling, progressing
But experiencing that of those above
Has been my greatest blessing